# Ups Bounce Dash

## Eilish Martin

*Eilish Martin*

SUMMER PALACE PRESS

First published in 2008 by

Summer Palace Press
Cladnageeragh, Kilbeg, Kilcar, County Donegal, Ireland

Printed by Nicholson & Bass Ltd.

A catalogue record for this book is available
from the British Library

ISBN 978-09552122-8-4

This book is printed on elemental chlorine-free paper

*for  Sean*

*and for*
*Oisín,  Emer and Sean Óg*

# Acknowledgments

Poems from this collection have appeared in *HU, Artwords* and *Artslink.* Some have featured in readings given at Aspects, The Donegal Bay and Bluestacks Festival, The Hewitt Spring School 2006 and The University of Lancashire Symposium on Irish Writing.

# Biographical Note

Eilish Martin was born in Belfast and continues to live there. Her first collection, *slitting the tongues of jackdaws*, was published in 1999 and translations of her poems have been published in Russia and Mexico. She has read in the Writers' Union and The British Council in St. Petersburg, Russia.

# CONTENTS

# The Cooler

Yes. I remember The Cooler,
its clinically clean aquamarine pool

its lifebelts empty red Os
on the perimeter

fencing. I went swimming there
in Summer weather

– miles you'd go, going nowhere
no matter how long you'd go,

and only the echoing drone
of a far, far away loudhailer,

*breathe (two, three, four) breathe –*


and yes, some may've
turned and given a wave

before disappearing off
on their own

having had enough of The Cooler,
of its chlorinated water

of all that gulping for air.

# Constant Enders

All whist and whirr
between two enders

turning rope
a line of girls

all sing-song
climbing air

birling round
touching ground

running through

past soldier, sailor,
rich man, poor,

past sticks and stones
past broken bones

past guns and drums
and drums and guns

past the wind, the wind,
the wind blowing high

past the rain coming
tumbling from the sky

past candy apples
hard green pears

past conversation
lozenges

all whist and whirr
between two enders

between two enders
all sing-song.

# Dawning

First light, and out we'd go into the snow
rejoicing, playing the fool
all the way to school.

Inside we rhymed off sing-song prayers,
the Catechism, rules of grammar,
weights and measures,

the beginning and ending years of wars,
all the time eyeing the high windows
longing for signs of more snow.

Hometime, and daylight all but gone
we'd be let go into a fresh fall,
mouths wide open,

in our glory, as sure of snow
lasting on stretched out tongues
as heaven above, and here below.

# Birthmark

The rules had been and always would be
– you were dead if you got touched
before reaching no man's land, and only one life each –

and if we played their way
then we could be the enemy.

But Mary McCormack, who was always short of breath
and couldn't run said one life was not enough

and said we girls would play if she could nurse
our wounded back to health

in her backyard lean-to
red-crossed with scarlet lipstick.

I was glad enough to have loose fire
injure me and fall with my hands in the air

to be there and have her lift my vest
and have her kiss the patch of puckered skin

between my shoulder blades
that could have been an exit wound.

# Primary Education

1

Miss Fitzsimmons had a garden
she'd reveal

in names of shrubs we'd never seen,

rhododendron, hydrangea,
camellia

or in varieties of trees,

upright trees, weeping trees,
trees with bark that peeled.


She brought their closed buds to school
for us to see them bloom.

In English time we copied out their muscular
names until our hands were fluent

and the skin grew tender
where it gripped the pen.


She gave out sheets of black sugar paper
creased down the middle

and coloured chalks and showed us
how to draw the flowers

keeping to the symmetry
of trumpets and chalices.

The chalk dust got everywhere
and gathered like sleep in our eyes.

2

History was in the telling of our names
– hers the offspring of a Norman squire

ours, the dragon's teeth
of Poyning's Law,

a class of renegade
beyond the pale

a class of absent Earl
taken to the air,

a class of poet
forever gone,

a class of rebel
hanged,

a class of straw-man
burned

and mine, the family name
of Castlereagh,

mad King George's
man –

O'Hanlon and McMahon,
O'Neill and O'Donnell Rua,

Hegerty, Orr, Lundy,
Stewart,

and migrant names that had taken here
like Fusco and Morelli.

All names she registered
in Irish

and called like those of flowers
we'd get to know,

names with wide throats
and red interiors,

names answered round the room
with, *Anseo! Anseo!*

3

One lunchtime I walked into a strange house
where there had been a death

and I remember how hard I tried
to hold my breath.

In the narrow room an old woman lay in her coffin
and everywhere was the smell of Jeyes Fluid.

A bluebottle flitted between her stone chin
and her stone forehead

and then rose, crisscrossing the small room,
and then drove itself home

lighting on the stone lips – a live
hook and eye doing up her mouth.

A priest called her, *our dearly departed
sister*, and said prayers for her and all the dead.

4

That year I learned how to carry numbers
and how to fetch them down

learned how to spell
by making sense of sound

learned to draw flowers
about a crease

learned my place
in history

learned that the living
concerned themselves with the dead

and death was unimpressed.

# First Principles

*in memory of Genevieve*

I look back through my sister's Senior Infants eyes
to see a name already made singular as Rousseau or Piaget.
Her shade, in sun-trapped fields of play
ringed round with breathless girls, all smiles
to find itself at one with Adam's rib, the bone
that is the be all and the end all of it all, the bone
the girls all sing out loud about
when they sing out
*the bone's all alone, the bone's all alone,*

and see her shade become the constant ender
ever running rings round break-time's giddy air
so flowing lines of rhyming girls can enter
with carry-on momentum, jumping clear
and landing, gladdened, fair and square.

# Morning Offering
*for Sister Rosaleen McMahon*

In the beginning we learned to reel
off prayers offering up our ups and downs, our baby work
stretched beyond its plasticine into the lo and behold
of a chance design, the smudged outline of a star,

its good-enough compass rose drawing us far
and wide (the rough and the ready and the bold)
as through a needle's eye into the soul's winding stair
and its daily office of desire

until we learned what our first parents learned on their quarter acre
east of Eden, squaring up to the holy and haunted nature
of clay – its humdrum play, its work-a-day prayer –
revelling in the lilies of the field, the birds of the air,

the *perpetuum mobile* of wheels within wheels
of a purpose who carved us for His seal.

# Dunlewey Street

*in memory of Sister Ita*

In tall rooms with windows to the floor
the first lesson was early morning light
across my desk and chalk dust dancing in mid-air

and moving in the dust and light through single
rows of girls, as if on air, a gracious habit
bending into my work
lifting it out of the dust on starched wings.

# Natural Disaster

Days break, small as little waves would break
on childhood days at Ballyholme or Waterfoot,
and on the edge of all, and only half awake,
I mostly let the days come in and let the days go out.

Some days though, I take the time to hunker down,
the way a child might do, and as a child curled low
wonder at what's left to wonder at – shell, stone, bone
bleached white, showing all they have to show,

and some days I take the time to look into the offing
my mother used to sing about when I was a child,
longing and longing over for something loving
returning out of the deep rolling sea and the wild.

# The Signalman

Standing over the levers he'd worked up with his spit
and a chamois leather, he'd scan the heavens for gear
shifts in the progress of clouds or the wheeling flight
of birds, divining in such things the speed of the weather
and if it foretold rain or shine. By his reading of the signs
outdoor work was begun or put off for the day,
washing was dried by the fire or hung in the open
and the young were given freedom to play.

He wrote a geography of his life in three jotters. On the cover
of Book 2 is written *Hartebees lefontein – fountain for beasts*
and also in his hand *Oxen to quench their thirst*
attributed to Shakespeare. That's where he's a Royal Dublin Fusilier
fighting the Boers. It starts with a hanky waving him off to war
and ends with, *best not knowing what the world has in store.*

# The Sugar Boiler
*in memory of Jack Stewart*

Under the masonry heads of Adam and Eve,
the stone fruits and flowers of paradise, the chiselled roses,
the pomegranates spilling seeds and show-off
leaves, hundreds, hushed hundreds of mortal faces
press against Jack's soul crossing into everlasting
life. And under the tongue's heartfelt *Amen* my fasting
mouth remembers jars of sucky sweets aglow
in clinched rows. And remembers lumps of honeycomb

dissolving down to honeycomb's sweet root
on nights when I was let stay up late
to watch – as through a glory hole into a furnace –
the give and take of grown-up company in our house
wrestling arms-wide-open skeins of airtight
sweetness into slabs of mouth-watering light.

# Crystal Set

The real thing was superfluous
to hope – that someone like Sean Hendron
from next door could spark voices
from the air. No matter, as it turned out, long
bursts of interference on his wireless
was all he got. Mere youngsters, hunkered
on our bottom step, we were a hair's
breadth away from the gift of tongues.

His plan for peace got him shot – crossing the Peace Line
in between the bombings and the shootings – its tissue
stretching ordinary heart to head, every sinew
in his grown hand outstretching a divine
idiocy – the makings of a down to earth promise
in the something and nothing of his voice.

# Small Mercies

Once – I almost said *once*
*upon a time* – our children's penny chews
were got from shops where bombs went off
or might've done. And once, grown-ups like us
weighed hope in ounces having lost enough
to know the heavens' far-fetched detritus,
falling here below, was down to chance
not providence. Not providence.

Some lost the names of those they loved (a torture
finding them all gone as through a door
swinging-to behind no all for-
giving last goodbye) and chanced upon a future
garden west of here – neat squares
of stiff grasses    of thrift    of paralysis.

# Look it
*for Ódhran*

Look it. This is all there is to it,

he'll come when the light's out
and you've turned your head away

– a redbreast flares in the corner of my eye –

and in the day you'll wake, all bright
and say out loud,

look it, he's been in the night
and left me something good.

# Ups Bounce Dash

Ups, full lick, all out,
upsy daisy

and bounce, all jar and jig
and juggle

and dash, kickback and rebound
and reverse.

The ways we learned
from one another

the jolt of smooth and broken
in the anatomy of shudder.

# Rhyming Time

When the butcher's shop
was blown up
cuts

of butcher's meat
were thrown over
rooftops

landing at the feet
of children
playing

ring-a-ring-
a-rosy in
Crimea Street.

Some let go hands
and turned
lame

from playing
children's
games,

others kept
the singing up
*a-husha*

*a-husha,*
*we all fall*
*down.*

# A Box of Tricks

Brought out to while away the fading hour,
her dayligone, between day bright and dark of night
when shadows ringing us around grew long and mightier
than her sing-song word for hushing the dying light,

her box of tricks – junk jewellery, a silky glove,
buttons, buckles, old greetings cards with loving words
and the letter x for kisses, *my darling Nan, dearest Nan, my love* –
her treasure trove, her crock of gold, her dragon's hoard.

For us an hour spent sorting stone from glass
from bone, trying on her rhinestone choker
her rolled gold chains, blowing ourselves the kisses
someone larger than life had meant for her.

# Remembrance Service

Winnie Hughes remembers the German prisoners of war
detained at Muckamore

being brought by truck to St. Comgall's
for Sunday Mass.

Choir-mistress and organist, she had leave
to speak to them

about the sung responses
and communion hymns.

*Panis Angelicus, Pange Lingua,* Gounod's *Ave Maria.*


She remembers one Christmas they brought a gift
for her, a crib of balsam wood with a wishing well

that swallowed up her face in glass
every time she made a wish.

She remembers her wartime husband,
a wireless operator in the Royal Signals,

being able to speak in long
and short flashes of sunlight

and how one Christmas in peacetime when setting up the crib
he told her of the voice imagined in his earpiece

intoning its vernacular *De Profundis* over the air,
after the fire-bombing of Dresden,

crying out of a desolate place,
*mein Gott, mein Frau und Kinder,*

and remembers how he'd never bother
with the crib's wishing well

– the way its looking glass
would blind his eyes.

# Change of Life

Between last Mass and Evening Devotions
Winnie Hughes, church organist,
choir mistress,

dance-band pianist in the summer season,
piano teacher, housewife
and mother

(answering to both her married
and maiden
names)

let fly her wedding delft, crashing
it to earth on the kitchen's
terrazzo floor

leaving her deep in smithereens
of weeping willow, small
pieces of Chinese

lovers and bits
of rickety
bridges

they'd spent a good part
of her married life
escaping across.

After Devotions she swept
her ruined delft
away

but for a curl of earthenware
scrolled like
a clef

that hurt her hand
when she made
a fist.

# Music Mistress

*With my eyes closed* – and you shout
as if I am the one who's hard

of hearing – *I can play the Moonlight*
*Sonata in my head.*

And your hurting hands begin
Beethoven's slow

movement across the bold roses
of your bedspread

mute as the words on my lips
your closed eyes will not read.

# Fugue

When I see you stroke
your throat

so lightly
with your right hand

I think of how the adjudicator
singled out your touch

when you were beginning the piano

and try to figure out
the unaware

action of your
left hand

– a nest
of alarms

and hunger
notes –

over and over
springing open

as if something
was being let go

weightless
into the air.

# Adagio

Caught in a slow
movement of light,
soundless as the words
on my lips,

in a breath
you return your shadow
to the wild,
alarmed

by your father's whistle
calling you home
across fields
of jaggy nettles.

# The Ends of the Earth

My brother Kevin was good with words, grand
names like Van Diemen's Land,
Tierra Del Fuego, Nova Scotia.

He used them like scaffolding
to dangle other words like
history and geography

as if condemning them to swing.

He knew words that gave him asthma.
Words like exploitation, conquest,
dispossessed,

and big words hard as lumps in his throat
that hurt just trying to say them,
like liberty and justice.

He was lifted in the 1950s and detained.
My father came back from the jail
speechless.

When Kevin was released
he took the £10 passage
to Australia.

At the Docks we waved him off
as if it was the start
of something big.

On the way home my father cried
to think of a son of his
having to ship off like that

to Van Diemen's Land.

# Heirloom

A Godmother's gift, its four square
whiteness weightless as the after
life a wing-beat leaves in gone-through air

– mindful of those souls gone before
into the light of love's labour,
its holding patterns of vanishing air –

a dowry, a bottom drawer, a future
prospect, its thread a continuous prayer
couched in the blessed-be of here

and now, the blessed-be of years before,
the blessed-be of happy ever after.

# Delivered

When I realised there was something wrong
the midwife did an ultrasound.
The gadget taking soundings found
a *Marie Celeste*, its cord of smoke twirling
skywards, disappearing with its log and crew's belongings
over the edge of the known world.

The consultant smiled down at me on the hospital couch
as though I'd survived some abominable triangle of ocean.
*Go home*, she said, as if I wouldn't be fetched
back to give birth – or at any rate go through the motions.

# Recovering

Here is a windfall some creature has eaten hollow as a snare
and here a seed, a brown teardrop its tongue has worked free
of the core. In its creamy heart it is the up-reach of winter
wood bearing the year's first snow, the year's first leafy
shoot, a bangle of blossom in Spring to bind the wrist
of a girl light-headed on a first glass of Calvados,
the year's first fruit coming away gorgeous
in the mouth between teeth and lips.

So like in some first garden before the coiled promise
sent our delinquent parents gaping with disbelief
into rented rooms papered with little words for death,
so cold they could see their own breath – only their delicious
kisses springing the other's mouth on the worst
of those small words, burning off some of their frost.

# Withstanding

At seven   these seven mornings   a song
*confederate of dawn*
nor stops   nor more   but one line   long

a small bird's song   all clean
and on   and on
at seven   theses seven mornings   a song

*confederate of dawn*
a risen song   nor stops
nor more   but one line   long

nor by the throat   nor done
(nor doing)   down
at seven   these seven mornings   a song

all rinse   all rung
all clean   a risen song
nor stops   nor more   but one line   long

nor by the throat   nor done   (nor doing)
down   and on   and on
*confederate of dawn*

at seven   these seven mornings   a song
nor stops   nor more
but one line   long.

# Joyful Mystery

In the half-light we hit our stride
along the excavated timbers of the pilgrims' road,

where the Annunciation is a beehive cell
waiting for the coming light,

where a flourish
in the air's a chitty wren, all flit and flight,

and where, above the Rosary's rise and fall
a cock-a-doodle-doo crows thrice,

though the Irish-speaking cockerel says,
*Tá Mac na hOighe slán,*

(the son of the Virgin is safe so).
And on we go, the day grown bright, buoyed

by the rush of sound and sense made flesh,
beside ourselves with joy.

# Winter Briefings

It's too late for the hazel wood
(like a mirror's silver gone)

too soon for the underpass,
its labyrinth dreaming long

shadows bringing me a thousand leagues
from home and back again

as though by wrist and ankle tied
to Ariadne's string.

Any day now I'll capture swirling legions
of returning birds

soaring like a hatch of zeros
out of the unexpected void

but in the meantime I'll go back
to the stored image

of a frozen bench in the gardens
of The Hermitage

that could be the equals sign
between two trees

of similar blackness, or the forced smile
of the word freeze.

# Brodsky's Living Room

To your left there is a door.
Look through its glass
into a room and a half

with the ambition of a cold eye
making something
of the present.

The owner of this room opposed
the words of politicians,
salesmen and charlatans.

Like a bird he chirped no matter
what twig he landed on
(we have his word for it)

and like the rest of us, could mistake
the rustle of leaves
for applause.

# January Aubade

Through a garden gate
and its iron zeros
asides of light

its simple progressions
its acts of life
its seraphic dialogue

bending into gone hollyhocks
gone ornamental
thistles.

# Vision Express

In this severe room, wired
for testing tired
eyes, the shadow
of a winter bird,
whose song remains,
sits in the corner of my eye
flitting from *nevermore* to *overawe*
hesitating between *snare* and *rare*.

Poor ghost
its yellowy beak coming clean
between the glittery boughs
overrun, yes, *overrun* with frost.

# Full Board

*in memory of Dorothy Hearne*

Standing inside the dark hall
missing her hanging rainproof,
her sun bonnet, her good-enough
bookcase against the wall, her tall
harp alive with woodworm – her stuff –
listening for an inside door
swinging-to behind
her determined balance.

All rush, a broad brush in one hand,
in the other a bucket of lime wash, this once
– without a house full of visitors
staying over, without furniture
slowing her – this once making light
of it all, leaving the place bright.

# Benediction

*for Ruth Carr*

My finger weighty
with gold for remembering
forgets entirely

the quiet way snow
has of lighting on stretched tongues
of melting the mouth.

# Summit

Out of a place where eyebright and juniper break
the Burren's limestone pavement,
the climber O'Donoghue, a hurley strapped to his back,
has climbed into a bare place without water
to drown him, wood to burn him or soil to bury him.

At this height, with a heart grown big as a baby's head
and a hurley big as the tree it was got from,
couldn't you stand a-sway the world
letting fly into its throat the Morrigan's rounded
prayer after the battle of Maigh Tuairead

*– peace up to the skies, the skies down to the earth,
the earth under the skies, strength to everyone.*

# Sightseeing at Carrera

Dante put these poker-playing quarrymen
into *The Inferno*. I swear in every face
all you'll ever need to know of bluff.

They've made it quits, picking out Dante's
words in monumental stone,
giving them a living.

The poet knew what he was doing, letting
his non-writing hand reach
into their futures

– labourers lowering the likes of Michaelangelo
into their quarry to feel for himself,
past its flaws and voids,

the marble's best muscle and bone, its gorgeous curls,
those already-there oversized hands
he just had to give to his David.

# One Day Return

The aircraft's tail light
climbs to its vanishing point
and out of sight.

Returning home,
clean above our heads
day-bright,

and our last born
lifted off into the light,

his flight outwitting
the goat-grey leavings of night.

# In Saecula Saeculorum

According to the law of oaths
an oath is sworn on seven sacred things.

Not then the heavens' darkling towers and stars
strung out like lamps

but seven words for Earth's
ordinary O

– growing fire
and growing snow –

words that slip like dew
into the sea

returning, when they do return,
with all the lovely broken things.

# Making Do

Pitching himself against the things he had to fix
and his own limitations
he'd bend into the work
of mending shoes, hammering home
the silvery sprigs issuing from his mouth

and once, mending a favourite board, split
along the soft flesh of its grain,
his tongue brought forth shiny squares
of corrugated steel to join the halves.

A good job too,
leaving behind three bright flashes
calling him to mind under the work
of breaking open loaves of bread
to offer round.

# Benchmark

By doubling over, folding in, opening out,
showing by division and sub-division
the increase in things worked at

his hands transformed yesterday's brief
news into wide-brimmed hats
for playing make-believe.

On holiday I do the same for his unknown
great-grandson, watching from a half-landing
– how he makes a world of his own,

makes the best of a dull
day – measuring his play
along a level cut into my skull.

# Christening
*for Tiarnán*

Eye-deep in stone we entered All Saints, cradling
in overlapping arms a small soul lovingly rocked to sleep,
passing below an arch upheld by air's geometry, spilling
ourselves into oblongs of light falling fathoms deep

underfoot. And looking up, an upturned boat, clinker-built,
riding above the baptismal font, and angels, all decked out, poured
into the helm, rocking the vessel through every compass point,
checking the needle's false north – each anointing
the other's hands with antique oils, ready to weigh anchor
and make off with us into heaven's orient.

# First Words

Because of who your mother is
you will need to know the word for
food, root, moon, blood,
the ocean's bosom.
The word for vowel.

Because of who your father is
you will have to know the word for
trapeze, tightrope, blindfold,
escapologist.
The word for consonant.

Because of who your grandfather is
you will need to know the word for
.mayfly, daddy-long-legs, grasshopper,
a watertight hold.
The word for syllable.

Because of who your grandmother is
you will have to know the word for
tongue, tongue-tied, breath
and the absence of breath.
The word for word.

# Generation Gap

Travelling home from minding our first grandson
the talk between us is all small talk, the house,
the garden, the weather up ahead,

but my mind is on Tiarnán in his wellingtons
and waterproof, the double of his dad
the day he stepped off into Lough Mask

(because of the carefree clouds riding the sky
swinging the livelong day on a hinge
of air and water)

and thinking this journey would not be happening
without you going out of your depth
to bring him back

without you wrapping him in your oilskin
to stop him from perishing
with the cold.

And only know we're home from minding
our small grandson when I hear
you sigh *Glory be!*

# Watercolour

There's a saying taken from the Irish,
*an ounce of care is worth a pound of cure.*

I heard a painting master say it to his beginners
and watched him make the watery edge
of his pictured world yield, as by its own accord.

At the water's edge of my grandsons' world
where they brush up against the Irish Sea,
I want what I say to them to be as wet on wet

– bog water, ditch water, water from an unsought
stone the old ones say will cure your ills –

so my words might fall fresh as the wash
of a broken wave catching them out
sending them running wild.

# No Rhyme nor Reason

Word-fast with birdsong and dandelion clocks
long into an afternoon

loving my grandson's soft-as-feathers
*bir, bir* for the liquid play of muscle and air

uplifting our faces
into light-headedness,

loving the embryonic
logic of his tongue's *tic-toc*

for the drift of hours loosed off
on curls of breath


until a wisp of dandelion fruit
startles his throat, leaving me without

words for his chuffed mouth
working it free in husky coughs.

# In his Element

Surfacing in the shallow end he's all off-guard,
surprised by himself, desiring more,

and because he will insist on going under
I show him how to hold his breath

how to go below, how to be a blur
underwater, a submerged shiver

muscling its way between
open ocean and gravel bed.

# On the Feast of the Epiphany

All day it is grey as dawn
and each of us is a Wiseman
on the shore at Cushendall

following a made-up star, bearing our small gifts thus far,
stones from the round stones on the beach,
a driftwood bestiary of creatures

from the Middle Ages, a head full of lonely thoughts
(the winter weather – its silver dropping below nought –
faith in what should be there).

The two boys are brave
believing in stones and driftwood and stars
to wish upon, and have no time to stare

at low horizons. I can barely hold them back
by the hoods of their anoraks
from walking on waves.

# Cemetery Sunday

This is the way we come, each a pilgrimage of one
facing into a cold name stood out in stone
remembrance, each with a bunch
of cut blooms, the same
as all the fallen-over ones
whose decomposing stench
our hands will carry home.
And then a prayer, and then we go

out between the staggered rows
of graves, arm in arm for fear of being lost
in gathering ghosts, lost in low
conversation about the cost
of burying the dead, counting each breath
counting off the dearly loved, beloved of death.